C is for CHAMPIONS

Written by Brandon Green   **Illustrated by Zoe Ranucci**

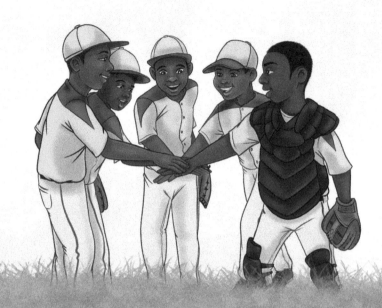

First Edition

Edited by Simply Green Educational Training and Consulting

Illustration and Design by Zoe Ranucci, www.GoodDharma.com

ISBN:978-0-578-84190-8

Library of Congress Control Number: 2021900888

SPECIAL THANKS TO...

This book is dedicated to Jaheim Benton, Cameron Bufford, D.J. Butler, Trey Hondras, Joshua Houston, Ed Howard, Marquis Jackson, Pierce Jones, Eddie King, Prentiss Luster, Lawrence Noble, Darion Radcliff my 2014 Little League teammates. We came, we played we won! May your life continue to be filled with championships.

A special thanks to my parents for preparing me to become a champion.

 is for
Courage

Choose to confront uncertainty
and continue to move forward
with your life in spite of obstacles.

is for Honesty

Always display
moral character that encourages
truthfulness and positivity.

is for
Ability

It's great to have raw talent,
however not everyone has it.
On and off the field you have to build
your skills which will ultimately separate you
and make you stand out above the rest.

is for
Motivation

This is your driving force. If you lack desire and determination, all other mental factors like confidence and emotion will cause your focus to become non-existent.

is for
Positivity

No matter the hand you are dealt,
you must adjust your mindset
to see yourself succeeding
and reaching your goals.

 **is for Integrity**

What will you do when no one is watching?
Displaying high levels of honesty
and responsibility is the surest way to
make your dreams come true.

is for
Opportunity

When you get the chance to do something,
you must approach it like it is the
last thing you will ever do.
Make people remember you
from any opportunity you receive.

is for
Never Quit

Baseball is the game of failure.
Failure is a part of life. However, you never
truly fail until you give up completely.
Don't follow your dreams, chase them.

is for
Success

Success comes in many sizes,
large and small. Setting up goals puts you
in position for these victories in life.

Brandon Green is currently a catcher at Southern University in Baton Rouge, Louisiana. Inspired by his father, he developed a love for baseball over fifteen years ago. This love has influenced his travel to over 30 states to play the sport.

His dedication and vision have not gone unrecognized. In 2014 Brandon was a member of the first all African-American Little League team to win the United States Little League World Series championship. Following this victory, Brandon and his teammates were the guest of former President Barack Obama and First Lady Michelle Obama in the White House Oval Office. He and some of his teammates were also featured in the August-September issue of Sports Illustrated. Brandon was also the guest of the Major League Baseball commissioner "Bud" Selig for the 2014 World Series. Chicago Magazine voted Brandon's 2014 championship team as the Chicagoan of the Year. Additionally, the Chicago White Sox ACE (Amateur City Elite) Baseball Club recognized Brandon's

2014 GRANT PARK CHAMPIONSHIP CELEBRATION PARADE, CHICAGO, IL

GAME #4 PRIME TIME

talents, and he was invited to become a select member of this elite organization. During the 2014 and 2015 season, Brandon received the honor of being voted player of the month by the White Sox ACE Baseball Club.

Brandon's off field attributes are equally matched by his athletic ability. He has trained with some of the best including former MLB player Lou Collier in his home town Chicago. In his spare time, Brandon enjoys photography, listening to and playing music. His favorite artist is Kendrick Lamar.

WHITE HOUSE VISIT NOVEMBER 2014

2014 GRANT PARK RALLY AFTER RETURNING FROM WILLIAMSPORT, PA

CPSIA information can be obtained
at www.ICGtesting.com
Printed in the USA
BVHW020108240321
602968BV00001B/13